# Books in the Linkers series

Homes discovered through Art & Technology
Homes discovered through Geography
Homes discovered through History
Homes discovered through Science

Myself discovered through Art & Technology
Myself discovered through Geography
Myself discovered through History
Myself discovered through Science

Toys discovered through Art & Technology
Toys discovered through Geography
Toys discovered through History
Toys discovered through Science

Water discovered through Art & Technology
Water discovered through Geography
Water discovered through History
Water discovered through Science

Food discovered through Art & Technology
Food discovered through Geography
Food discovered through History
Food discovered through Science

Journeys discovered through Art & Technology
Journeys discovered through Geography
Journeys discovered through History
Journeys discovered through Science

Reprinted 2002
First paperback edition 1996
First published 1996 in hardback by A&C Black Publishers Limited
37 Soho Square, London W1D 3QZ
www.acblack.com

ISBN 0-7136-4602-0
A CIP catalogue record for this book is available from the British Library.

Copyright © 1996 BryantMole Books

Commissioned photographs by Zul Mukhida
Artwork by Malcolm Walker
Design by Jean Wheeler

**Acknowledgements**

The publishers would like to thank the following organizations for supplying some of the toys used in this book: The
Africa Trading Company, Brighton; 6 (right), 10/11 (centre), 14/15 (centre), 19 (left), Anada, Brighton; 9 (right).
Picture acknowledgements: Chapel Studios; 4 (right), 16 (top), Robert Opie; 4 (left), 12 (left), 17, 19 (right).

A & C Black uses paper produced with elemental chlorine-free pulp,
harvested from managed sustainable forests

Printed and bound in Italy by L.E.G.O.

# Toys

## discovered through
## Geography

Karen Bryant-Mole

## <u>Contents</u>

**A & C Black • London**

# Toys around the world

Children all around the world play with toys.

Toys like this car are found in many parts of the world.

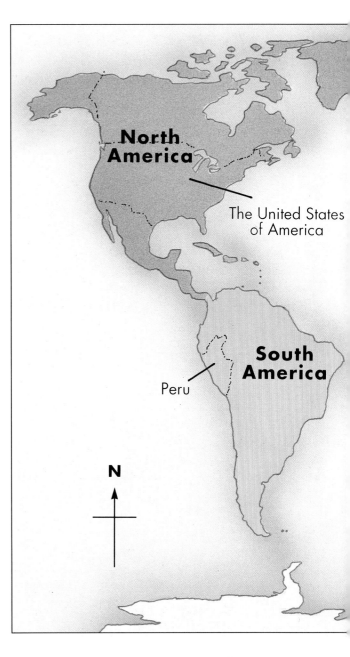

North America

The United States of America

South America

Peru

N

Other toys are special to one part of the world.

Our world is round, like a ball.
This map of the world is a flat drawing that shows you the position of the land and sea.

The Czech Republic

The Russian Federation

Britain

**Europe**

**Asia**

Japan

China

**Africa**

India

Ghana

Sri Lanka

Singapore

Java

**Oceania**

Australia

**Antarctica**

The world is divided up into seven areas, called continents. Most of the continents are made up of countries.

What country do you live in?
What continent is your country in?
Can you find that continent on the map?

As you go through the book you could use this map to see where each toy was made.

# Kites

Although kites are flown all over the world, it is in Asia that they are most popular and important.

### Kite day
In an Asian country called China, there is a special day for flying kites. Some of the kites look like butterflies. Others look like birds, people, dragons, fish or snakes.

### Boy's day
Japan is another Asian country. On May 5th, families in Japan fly paper carp outside their homes.

A carp is a type of fish. It is a very strong swimmer. One paper carp is flown for every boy in the family.

**Stunt kites**
This European kite has two handles.
It can be made to loop around in the air.
It can swoop and dive.

Kites like this can now be bought in many places around the world.

# Dolls

Dolls can be made from different materials.

## Plastic

This doll is made from a type of plastic, called vinyl. Vinyl is made in factories all over the world.

## Wood

Dolls can also be made from materials that grow in a particular area.

This African doll has been carved from wood. The wood comes from a tree that grows in many African countries.

## Maize

These two dolls have been made from maize husks.

Maize is grown in lots of countries, especially countries in Europe and North America.

7

# Puppets

Puppets are often used to act out stories that have been told for hundreds of years.

**Glove puppets**
Some puppets are worked by putting your hand inside the puppet.

These puppets tell the story of Punch and Judy. It is a story that is told in many European countries.

## String puppets
The Asian puppet on the left comes from a country called Sri Lanka. The puppet is wearing traditional Sri Lankan clothes. It is worked by strings.

## Rod puppets
This puppet comes from another part of Asia, called Java. He is worked by thin rods.

9

# Board games

Many games have playing pieces and some type of board.

## Ludo

This game is played by rolling a dice and moving counters on the board.

Games that are won or lost by the throw of a dice are sometimes called games of chance.

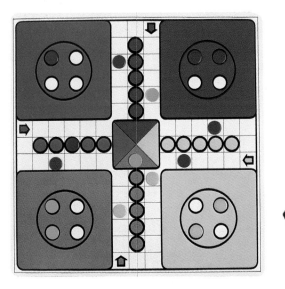

## Oware

This game comes from the African country, Ghana, where it is known as oware.
Games like oware are played in many African and Asian countries.
Oware is a game of skill. The more you practise at the game, the more likely you are to win.

## Chopat

This Asian game has many names.
In parts of India it is called Chopat.
It is very like the game of Ludo.
Instead of throwing a dice,
the players throw cowrie shells.

How do you play
your favourite
board game?

# Wooden toys

For thousands of years, wood has been used to make toys.

**Hand-carved**

This hand-carved bear was made in Russia. Can you find the Russian Federation on the map at the beginning of this book?

When the ball hanging below the bear is swung, the bear moves his arms and looks as though he is fishing.

## Machine-carved

This toy was carved by machine. It was made in a European country called the Czech Republic.
As the toy is pulled along, the wheels turn and the man's feet go up and down.

## Painted

All around the world, young children play with wooden building blocks. These blocks have been painted.

Some blocks are the colour of natural wood.

# Baby toys

Around the world you can find different versions of the same type of baby toys.

**Cot mobile**
This cot mobile comes from India, in Asia.
It is made from cotton with brightly coloured threads that sparkle as the toy turns.

**Rattle**
Here is an African rattle. It is made from large seed-heads filled with beans.

**Activity centre**
This plastic toy has lots of
different activities to keep
a baby amused.
Activity centres like this
are made and sold in many
continents.

# Toys on wheels

Toys that move are popular all over the world.

## Cart
The Indian boy in this picture is playing with a home-made cart.

Many families around the world can't afford expensive toys. Children can have just as much fun with home-made toys.

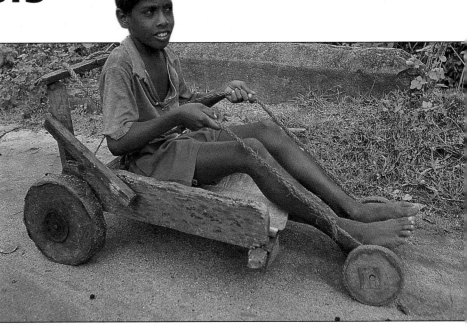

## Skateboards
Skateboards were invented in North America.

Now they are popular in many other continents, particularly Europe and Oceania.

## Truck

Here is another home-made toy.
This truck was made in Africa from
an old oil drum.

Home-made toys are often made
from materials that people
have thrown away.

Do you have any toys
on wheels?

17

# Noisy toys

No matter where they live, almost all children like making a noise!

**Trumpet**
This plastic toy trumpet was made in Britain. Toy instruments are played in other European countries and all over the world.

## Drums

These child-sized drums come from Africa.

Animal skins have been stretched over the top of the drums.

## Flute

Here is a South American flute from a country called Peru.

It is made of clay and is shaped like a goat.

19

# New toys

Some types of toy have been invented quite recently.

**Computer**
This computer was made in the United States of America.

Many computers and computer games are made in this North American country.

## Radio-controlled car

The radio-controlled car below was made in an Asian country called Singapore.

Lots of radio-controlled toys are made in Asia.

## Talking doll

This talking doll was made in an Asian country, too.

Many Asian factories have very modern equipment.

# National toys

Although many toys can be found the world over, some toys come from one particular country.

### Matroyshka
These wooden dolls come from the Russian Federation. They fit inside one another.

They are often called Russian nesting dolls but their proper name is Matroyshka.

## Boomerang

This is a plastic boomerang.
Wooden boomerangs were
used as hunting tools by
aborigines in Australia.
Australia is in Oceania.

Today the boomerang is
mostly used as a toy.
When it is thrown, it flies
back to the thrower.

## Cricket

Here is a child's cricket set.
Cricket is a ball game that began
in Britain.

It is also played in many of the
countries that were once ruled
by Britain.

# Glossary

**cot mobile**   a toy that is hung over a cot to keep a baby amused
**equipment**   things that are used for a particular purpose; in a factory these might be machines or tools
**instrument**   something used to make musical sounds
**invent**   think of or make something new
**maize**   a plant that is often called sweetcorn or Indian corn
**materials**   what objects are made from
**position**   where something is

# Index

## How to use this book

Each book in this series takes a familiar topic or theme and focuses on one area of the curriculum: science, art and technology, geography or history. The books are intended as starting points, illustrating some of the many different angles from which a topic can be studied. They should act as springboards for further investigation, activity or information seeking.

The following list of books may prove useful.

## Further books to read

| Series | Title | Author | Publisher |
| --- | --- | --- | --- |
| Around the World | Toys and Games | Godfrey Hall | Wayland |
| Beans | all Geography titles | various | A&C Black |
| Our Country | all titles | various | Wayland |
| | Picture Atlas for Children | Nicholas Price & Julia Garton | George Philip |